30 Nursery Rhymes

with sheet music and fingering for

Tin Whistle

Stephen Ducke

To download the audio files for this book, see
http://wfk.tradschool.com

Arrangements by Stephen Ducke
Web www.tradschool.com
Email info@tradschool.com

Contents

Oh, Dear, What Can The Matter Be?

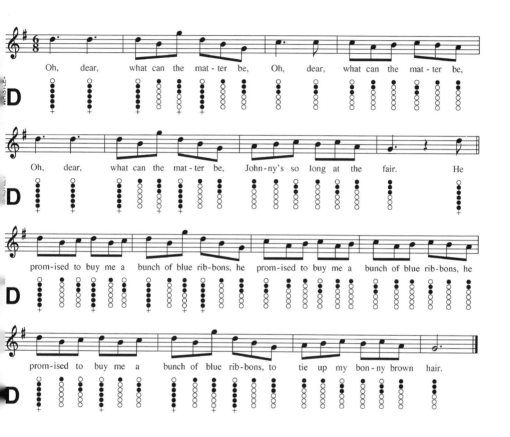

Old King Cole

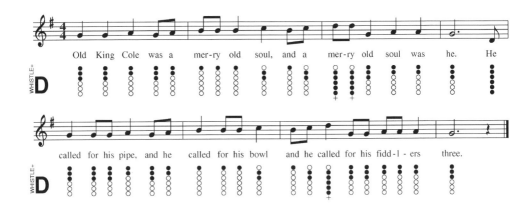

Old King Cole was a mer-ry old soul, and a mer-ry old soul was he. He called for his pipe, and he called for his bowl and he called for his fidd-l-ers three.

Old King Cole was a merry old soul,
And a merry old soul was he;
He called for his pipe,
And he called for his bowl,
And he called for his fiddlers three.
Every fiddler had a fiddle,
And a very fine fiddle had he.
Oh there's none so rare as can compare
With King Cole and his fiddlers three.

Baa, Baa, Black Sheep

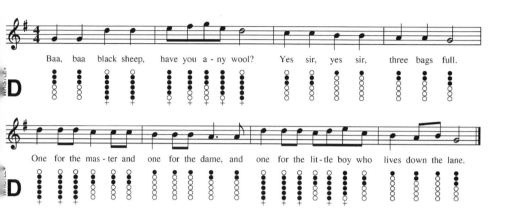

Baa, baa black sheep, have you a - ny wool? Yes sir, yes sir, three bags full.

One for the mas - ter and one for the dame, and one for the lit - tle boy who lives down the lane.

The Mulberry Bush

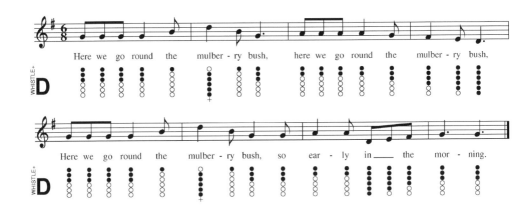

Here we go round the mulber - ry bush, here we go round the mulber - ry bush,

Here we go round the mulber - ry bush, so ear - ly in ___ the mor - ning.

Row, Row, Row Your Boat

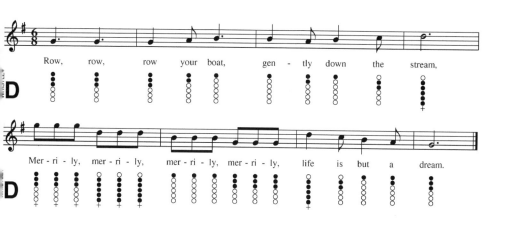

Twinkle, Twinkle, Little Star

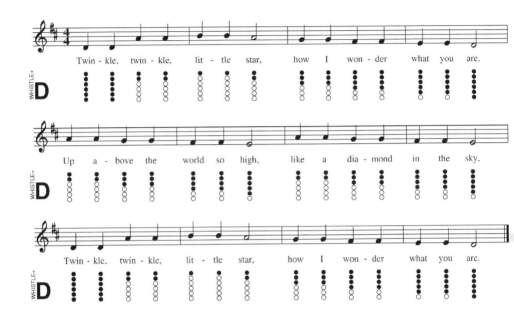

Twin - kle, twin - kle, lit - tle star, how I won - der what you are.

Up a - bove the world so high, like a dia - mond in the sky,

Twin - kle, twin - kle, lit - tle star, how I won - der what you are.

Rock-a-bye Baby

Rain, Rain, Go Away

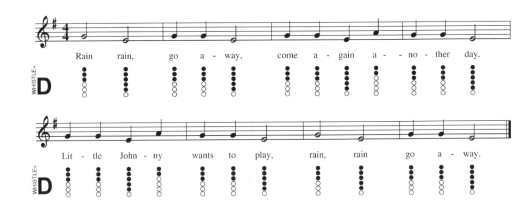

WHISTLE+ D

Rain rain, go a - way, come a - gain a - - no - ther day.

WHISTLE+ D

Lit - tle John - ny wants to play, rain, rain go a - way.

Ten Little Indians

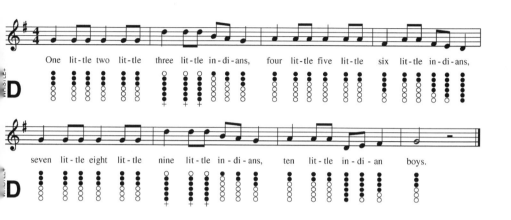

One lit-tle two lit-tle three lit-tle in-di-ans, four lit-tle five lit-tle six lit-tle in-di-ans,

seven lit-tle eight lit-tle nine lit-tle in-di-ans, ten lit-tle in-di-an boys.

Three Blind Mice

Hush Little Baby

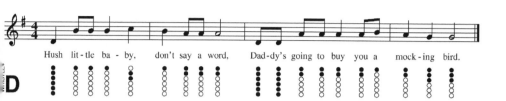

Hush lit‑tle ba‑by, don't say a word, Dad‑dy's going to buy you a mock‑ing bird.

Hush, little baby, don't say a word,
Daddy's gonna buy you a mockingbird.
And if that mockingbird won't sing,
Daddy's gonna buy you a diamond ring.
And if that diamond ring turns to brass,
Daddy's gonna buy you a looking glass.
And if that looking glass gets broke,
Daddy's gonna buy you a billy goat.

And if that billy goat won't pull,
Daddy's gonna buy you a cart and bull.
And if that cart and bull turn over,
Daddy's gonna buy you a dog named Rover.
And if that dog named Rover won't bark.
Daddy's gonna buy you a horse and cart.
And if that horse and cart fall down,
You'll still be the sweetest little baby in town.

The Grand Old Duke of York

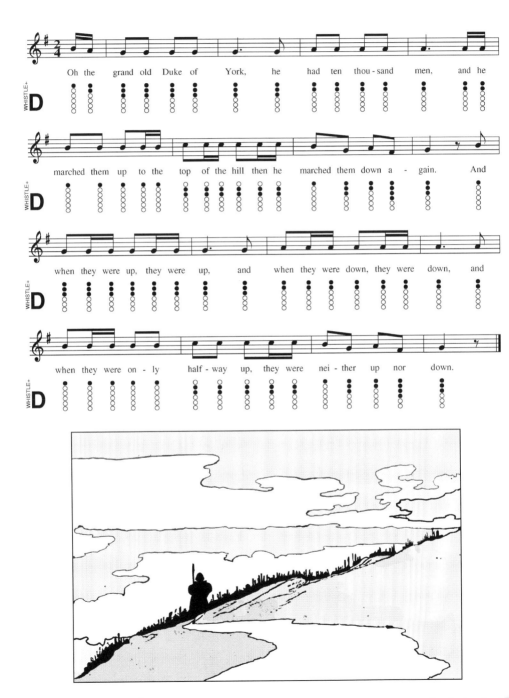

Mary Had a Little Lamb

Mary had a little lamb,
Little lamb , little lamb ,
Mary had a little lamb,
Its fleece was white as snow.

Everywhere that Mary went,
Mary went, Mary went,
Everywhere that Mary went,
The lamb was sure to go.

Head, Shoulders, Knees and Toes

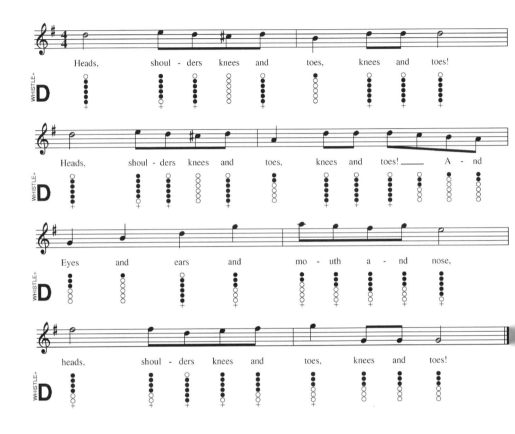

Bingo

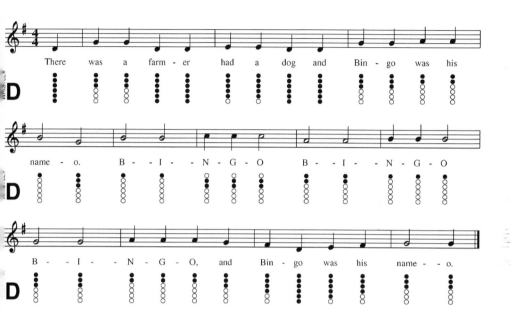

There was a farm-er had a dog and Bin-go was his

name - o. B - I - N - G - O B - I - N - G - O

B - I - N - G - O, and Bin-go was his name - o.

There was a farmer had a dog,
And Bingo was his name-o.
(Clap)-I-N-G-O! (Clap)-I-N-G-O!
(Clap)-I-N-G-O!
And Bingo was his name-o!
There was a farmer had a dog,
And Bingo was his name-o.
(Clap, clap)-N-G-O! (Clap, clap)-N-G-O!
(Clap, clap)-N-G-O!
And Bingo was his name-o!

There was a farmer who had a dog,
And Bingo was his name-o.
(clap)-(clap)-(clap)-G-O...
There was a farmer who had a dog,
And Bingo was his name-o.
(clap)-(clap)-(clap)-(clap)-O... etc
There was a farmer who had a dog,
And Bingo was his name-o.
(clap)-(clap)-(clap)-(clap)-(clap)... etc

Oranges and Lemons

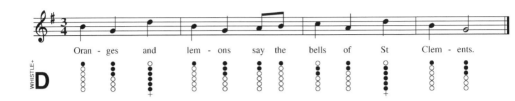

Oran - ges   and   lem - ons   say   the   bells   of   St   Clem - ents.

WHISTLE+

D

Oranges and lemons,
Say the bells of St. Clement's.

You owe me five farthings,
Say the bells of St. Martin's.

When will you pay me?
Say the bells of Old Bailey.

When I grow rich,
Say the bells of Shoreditch.

When will that be?
Say the bells of Stepney.

I do not know,
Says the great bell of Bow.

Here comes a candle to light you to bed,
And here comes a chopper to chop off your head.

Bobby Shaftoe

Bob - by Shaf - toe's gone to sea_____ sil - ver buc - kles at his knee._____

He'll come back to mar - ry me,_____ Bon - ny Bob - by Shaf - toe.

Bob - by Shaf - toe's bright and fair, combing out his yel - low hair,

He's my love for ev - er more, Bon - ny Bob - by Shaf - toe.

This Old Man

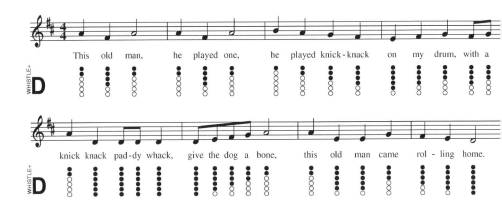

This old man, he played one,
He played knick-knack on my thumb;
With a knick-knack paddywhack,
Give the dog a bone,
This old man came rolling home.

This old man, he played two,
He played knick-knack on my shoe;
With a knick-knack paddywhack,
Give the dog a bone,
This old man came rolling home.

This old man, he played three,
He played knick-knack on my knee;
With a knick-knack paddywhack,
Give the dog a bone,
This old man came rolling home.

This old man, he played four,
He played knick-knack on my door;
With a knick-knack paddywhack,
Give the dog a bone,
This old man came rolling home.

This old man, he played five,
He played knick-knack on my hive;
With a knick-knack paddywhack,
Give the dog a bone,
This old man came rolling home.

This old man, he played six,
He played knick-knack on my sticks;
With a knick-knack paddywhack,
Give the dog a bone,
This old man came rolling home.

This old man, he played seven,
He played knick-knack up in heaven;
With a knick-knack paddywhack,
Give the dog a bone,
This old man came rolling home.

This old man, he played eight,
He played knick-knack on my gate;
With a knick-knack paddywhack,
Give the dog a bone,
This old man came rolling home.

This old man, he played nine,
He played knick-knack on my spine;
With a knick-knack paddywhack,
Give the dog a bone,
This old man came rolling home.

This old man, he played ten,
He played knick-knack once again;
With a knick-knack paddywhack,
Give the dog a bone,
This old man came rolling home.

Ten Green Bottles

Old MacDonald

Old Mac Don - ald had a farm, e - i - e - i - - oh, and

on that farm he had a cow, e - i - e - i - - oh, with a

moo - moo here and a moo - moo there, here a moo, there a moo, ev - ery - where a moo - moo

Old Mac Don - ald had a farm, e - i - e - i - - oh.

And on that farm he had a dog...
With a "bow-wow" here...

And on that farm he had some
sheep...
With a "baa baa" here...

And on that farm he had a pig...
With an "oink-oink" here...

And on that farm he had some
hens...
With a "cluck-cluck" here...

Little Bo Peep

Lit - tle Bo Peep has lost her sheep, and does-'nt know whe - re to find them.

Leave them a - lone, and they will come home, wag-ging their tails ___ be - hind them.

Polly Put the Kettle On

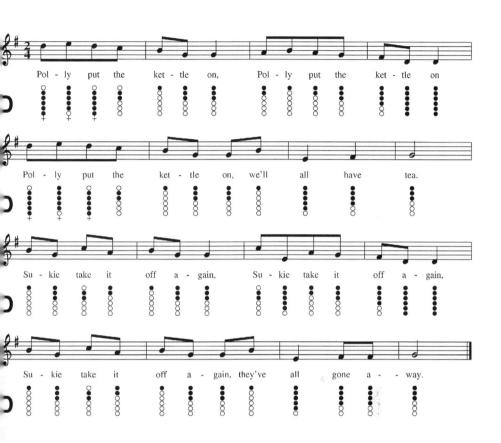

Pol - ly put the ket - tle on, Pol - ly put the ket - tle on

Pol - ly put the ket - tle on, we'll all have tea.

Su - kie take it off a - gain, Su - kie take it off a - gain,

Su - kie take it off a - gain, they've all gone a - - way.

Hey Diddle Diddle

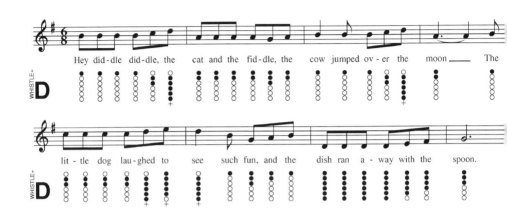

Hey did-dle did-dle, the cat and the fid-dle, the cow jumped ov-er the moon___ The

lit-tle dog lau-ghed to see such fun, and the dish ran a-way with the spoon.

he Wheels on the Bus

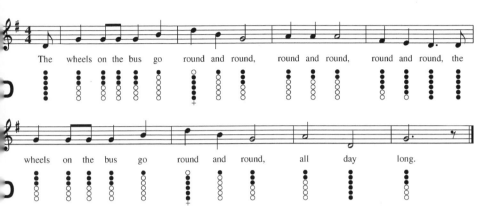

The wheels on the bus go round and round, round and round, round and round, the wheels on the bus go round and round, all day long.

The horn on the bus goes beep, beep, beep...

The people on the bus go chatter, chatter, chatter ...

The baby on the bus goes wah, wah, wah...

The bell on the bus goes ding, ding, ding...

The Muffin Man

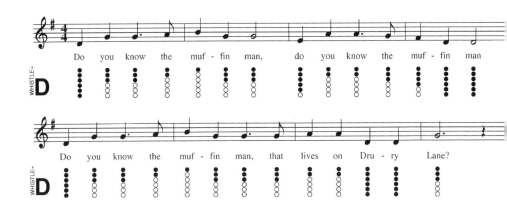

Do you know the muf - fin man, do you know the muf - fin man

Do you know the muf - fin man, that lives on Dru - ry Lane?

Yes, I know the muffin man,
The muffin man, the muffin man,
Yes, I know the muffin man,
That lives on Drury Lane.

Eensy Weensy Spider

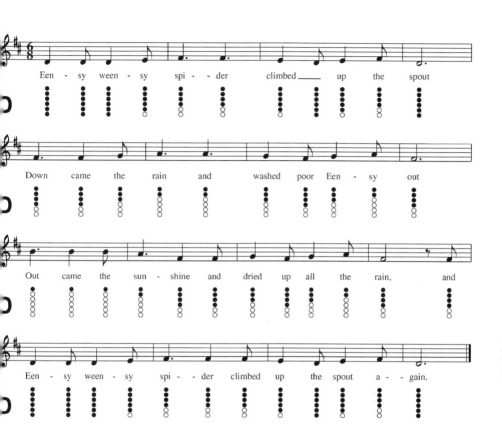

Een - sy ween - sy spi - - der climbed ___ up the spout

Down came the rain and washed poor Een - sy out

Out came the sun - shine and dried up all the rain, and

Een - sy ween - sy spi - - der climbed up the spout a - - gain.

Sing a Song of Sixpence

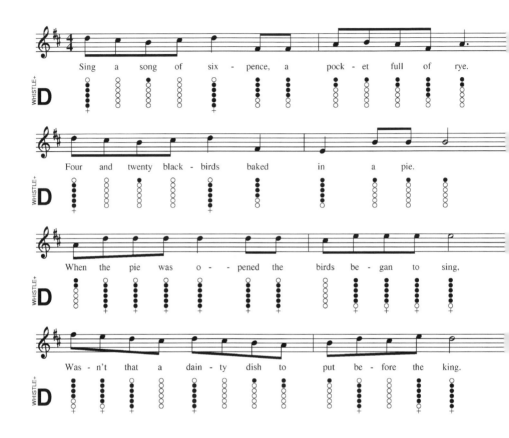

Sing a song of six - pence, a pock - et full of rye.

Four and twenty black - birds baked in a pie.

When the pie was o - - pened the birds be - gan to sing,

Was - n't that a dain - ty dish to put be - fore the king.

One Man Went to Mow

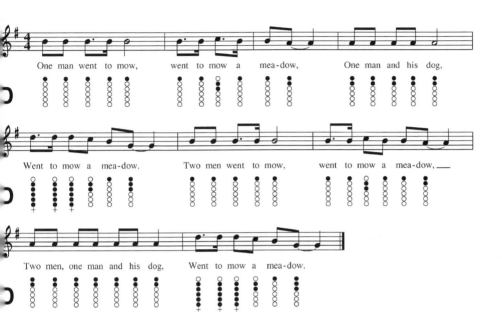

Three Little Kittens

Hot Cross Buns

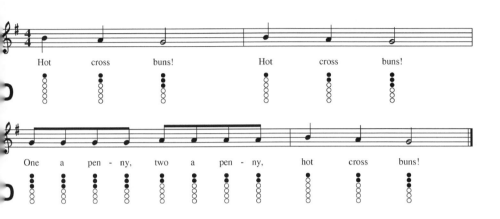

Appendix : Playing the Tin Whistle

You will find in the following pages some basic information to help you begin playing the tunes in this book on the whistle.

Holding the whistle

The whistle has 6 holes, which are covered with the first three fingers of each hand. The left hand fingers cover the top three holes, while the right hand covers the bottom (if you're left-handed, you may feel more comfortable with the right hand on top).

Grip the tip of the mouthpiece firmly between the lips (not the teeth) and rest the barrel on the thumbs; if held firmly at the mouthpiece, it shouldn't move. To make a sound, hold the whistle without covering any holes and blow a long, steady stream of air.

Tablatures & playing your first notes

In the tablatures that accompany the airs in this collection, the 6 holes of the whistle are represented by a diagram; open holes are indicated by white circles, while closed holes are black.

To play your first notes on the whistle, start with the C# (C sharp) which is played all holes open.

Then lower one finger at a time, starting with the left index (on the hole nearest the mouthpiece of the whistle) as in the diagram below:

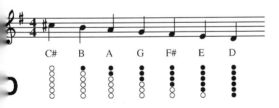

Be careful that the holes are properly covered, but without clenching the whistle too tightly - this will take some practise at the start. If a certain note doesn't play (or makes a squeaking or squeaking sound) then it is probably because a hole is not properly covered and leaking air. If this happens, start at the top again and come back down.

The first octave

Here are all the notes of the first octave, starting with low D:

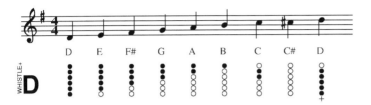

The second octave

To play the second or higher octave, the fingering doesn't change except for the high D. For all other notes, you just need to blow slightly harder. On the fingering tablatures, the second octave is indicated by the plus symbol.

For the tunes in this collection, there is no need to play higher than the high B.

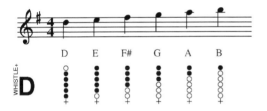

The scale of D

Here is the scale of D :

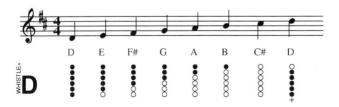

The scale of G

Here is the scale of G, with one new note, C natural.

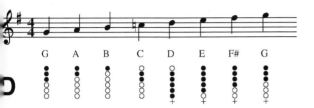

Here is the complete range of notes you will play on the tin whistle

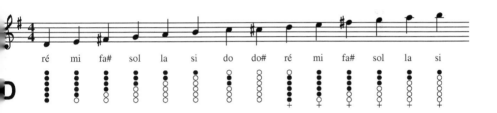

THE TUNEBOOK SERIES

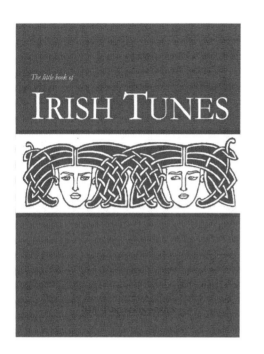

The little book of

IRISH TUNES

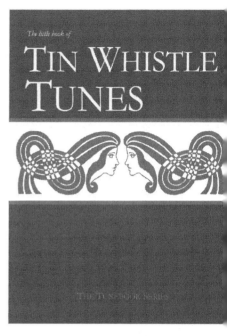

The little book of

TIN WHISTLE TUNES

The little book of

CELTIC MUSIC

The little book of

IRISH SONGS

TIN WHISTLE FOR BEGINNERS

Tin Whistle for Beginners : easy Irish songs and Tunes with fingering guides for Tin Whistle

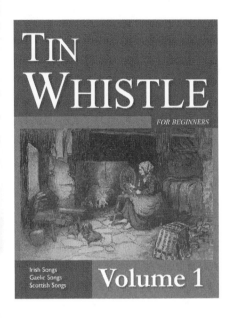

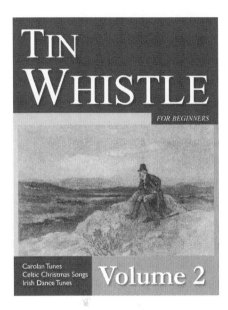

Whistle for Kids : easy tin whistle tunes for children

ALSO AVAILABLE

Irish Music - 400 Traditiona Tunes

184 pages, with audio download

Classic Irish Session Tunes from the author of "A Complete Guide to Playing Irish Traditional Music on the Whistle". A unique collection of the most popular tunes played in Ireland ... and throughout the world. Complete with 400-track audio download of each tune played at moderate speed on Tin Whistle.

Stephen Ducke is an Irish flute and whistle playe: from County Roscommon. Musician for over 30 years and an inspired teacher, he has recorded on solo album and is author and editor of several books of Irish and traditional music.

A Complete Guide to Playing Irish Traditional Music on the Whistle

286 pages; with 429 accompanying au tracks

This tutor book, with its accompanying audio file intended to give a complete introduction to playi Irish music in the traditional style on the tin whis it covers all from the very first notes on the instruments to the most advanced ornamentation.

It is intended for anybody who wants to play traditional music in the Irish style, from complete beginners to confirmed or advanced players who wish to work on their style or ornamentation. Tablature as well as sheet music is used througho the book, so it is accessible to the complete begir while more advanced players will appreciate the attention to detail in style and ornamentation in t later parts of the book.

Made in the USA
Middletown, DE
20 September 2022